murdoch
children's
research
institute

ABN 21 006 566 9782

Address: Murdoch Children's Research Institute
Royal Children's Hospital
Flemington Road, Parkville Victoria 3052 Australia
Email: hello@sleepwithkip.com
Website: www.sleepwithkip.com

1

Hello! Thanks for choosing a Kip book.

Based on over two decades of research, these books are here to help your child (and you) manage some common sleep problems children have.

There's loads of advice out there about how to help children sleep, and at the Murdoch Children's Research Institute in Melbourne, Australia, we pride ourselves on generating and sharing the advice you need based on evidence and research. This advice is now captured in the Kip books.

This series of six books is all about the common sleep problems in children, how your child can help themselves tackle them, and how you can manage them. Most are what we call 'behavioural' sleep problems (like getting to sleep, waking up overnight or waking up early).

As a paediatrician and researcher, I have seen over my 20 year journey, how much of an impact poor sleep in babies and children had on them as well as their parents. I met so many parents who were desperate for a good night's sleep! So I hope you find this book fun and helpful, for you, your child, your family and your friends.

Enjoy and sleep well!
Prof Harriet Hiscock

The Old Bedtime PASS PUNCHER

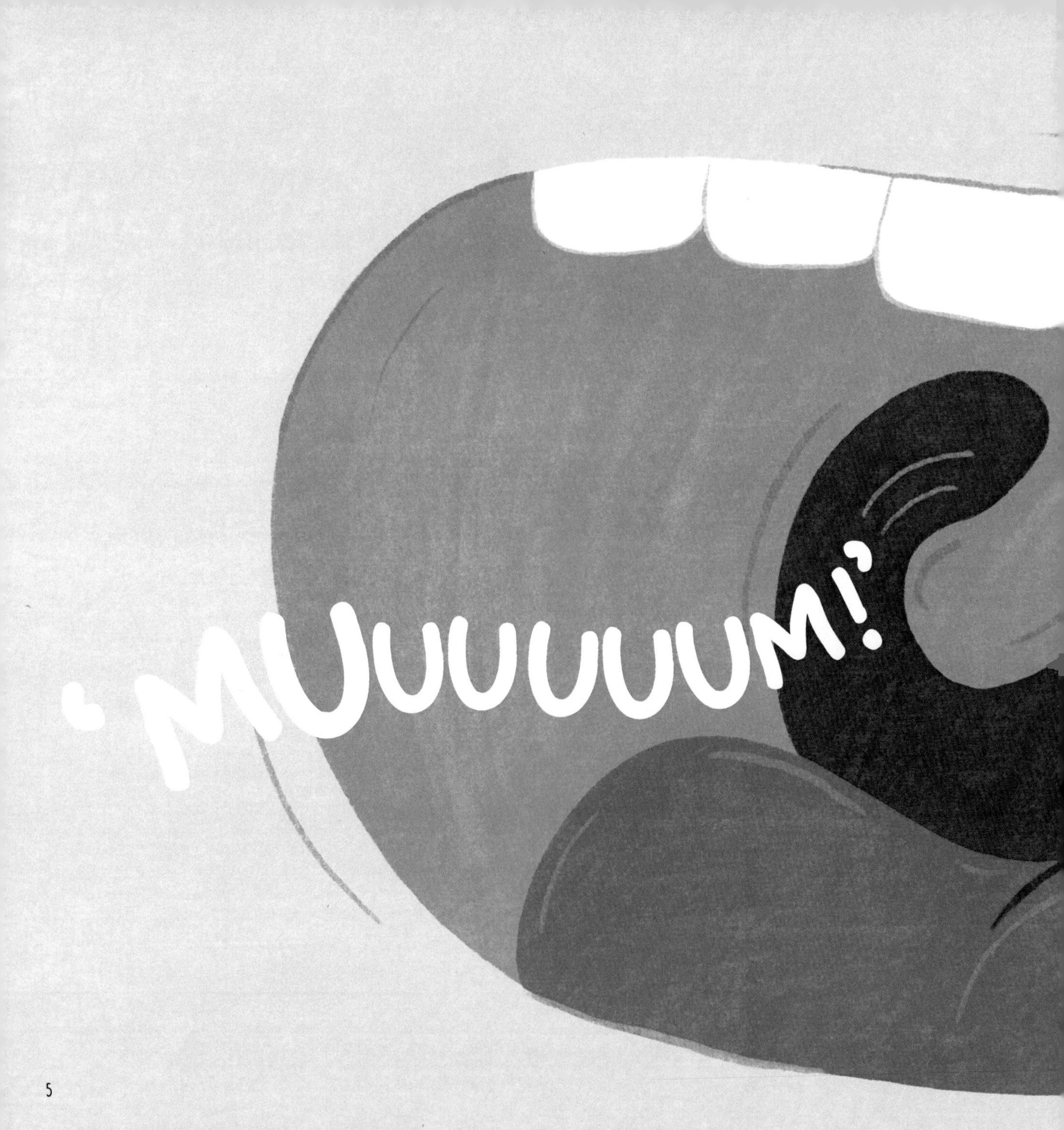
'MUUUUUUUM!'

'My knees are **itchy!**'

'I've lost my **teddy!**'

'Just one more **cuddle!**'

'I want to get up,
but my parents say
I need to sleep.
I just want a
few little things,'
said Molly.

10

'What **you need** is a **bedtime pass**, from my **good friend**...'

'...the Old Bedtime
  Pass Puncher.'

'Well **dengledee-doodlelee,**
hello there Molly!'

'I'm the Old Bedtime
Pass Puncher!'

'And here's your very, **own bedtime pass.**'

BEDTIME PASS

SINGLE

'What's a **bedtime pass?**' asked Molly.

'**Fimbledee-wimbles!**
Why, it's like a train ticket
for your **bedroom!**

BEDTIME
PASS

If **you want** to get up,
you just **say the word**
and I'll **punch** your **ticket.'**

'But you can **only use it once.** So **use** it **wisely.**'

'I think I need Dad to check my closet.'

CLOSETVILLE
'Whangleybangle, what an idea! He can check all the closets...'

'...and **wrestle your clothes,** as long as **you don't** need to **wee.**'

'Oh, you're right!
Maybe I'll go
for a wee.'

'Tingo-tango,
let's go for a wee!
The biggest,
hugest wee
of your life!'

'You'll **wee** like a **tap spills** out water.'

'Water! Maybe I should get a glass of water.'

'A lake!'

'An entire lickety-spickety ocean!'

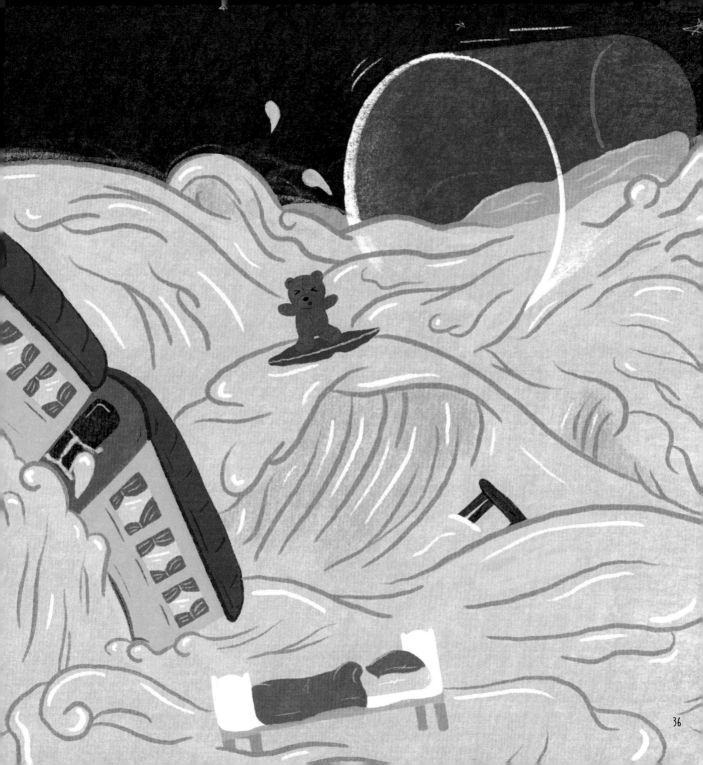

'More water than you **can** fit in a sandwich.'

SINGLE

BEDTIME PASS

'Burgers made of burgers. Chocolate chips. Chip chocolates.'

'Hmmm, I wonder **what Mum is doing.** Maybe I could **sit and watch TV with her?'**

'Yibber-yabber-yobber-yoo,
now there's an idea!'

'We can be adults
for an evening.

We can paint
our nails!'

'Watch movies where people kiss!'

SMOOCHBURG

49

'Make **important**
business calls,
and...'

'Actually,
Mr Old Bedtime
Pass Puncher...'

'...I've really
thought about it

and I want a
cuddle from Mum.'

'That **sounds** like a **great idea.**'

'Goodnight Molly.'

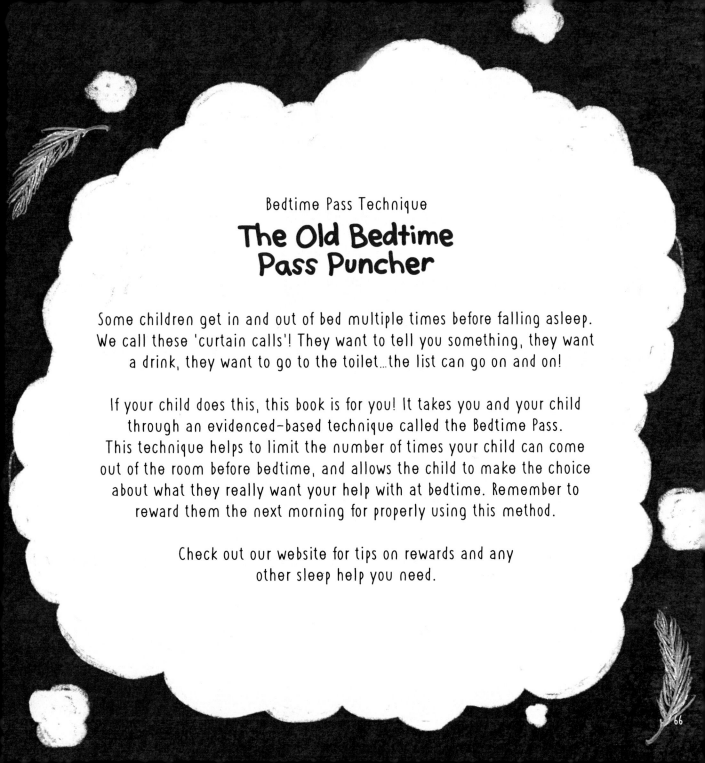

Bedtime Pass Technique

The Old Bedtime Pass Puncher

Some children get in and out of bed multiple times before falling asleep. We call these 'curtain calls'! They want to tell you something, they want a drink, they want to go to the toilet...the list can go on and on!

If your child does this, this book is for you! It takes you and your child through an evidenced-based technique called the Bedtime Pass. This technique helps to limit the number of times your child can come out of the room before bedtime, and allows the child to make the choice about what they really want your help with at bedtime. Remember to reward them the next morning for properly using this method.

Check out our website for tips on rewards and any other sleep help you need.

Also available in the Kip book series

Pick your
Own Nose

Slug Dad &
Monster Mum

Marshmallow Puffins
at the Window

Has Dad joined
the Circus?

A Beach in
the Bedroom

Murdoch Children's Research Institute is a not-for-profit organisation and the largest child health research institute in Australia. Their dedicated team of more than 1200 talented researchers is united to better understand, prevent and treat childhood conditions, helping to give all children the opportunity to live healthy and fulfilled lives.

For more than 35 years, the Murdoch Children's has been leading collaborations with national and international partners, policymakers, and health practitioners, to ensure that the benefits of its research are translated into real therapies and policies that improve the health and wellbeing of children all around the world, from preconception through to early adulthood.

Be sure to check out our website www.sleepwithkip.com and do the free Child Sleep Check to see what types of sleep problems your child may be experiencing and how you might be best able to help them.

murdoch
children's
research
institute

41340414R00038